KU-777-647

THE NINETIES COLLECTION

New Scottish Tunes in Traditional Style

by

Contemporary Scottish Composers

Edited by Ian Hardie

CANONGATE BOOKS
in association with
TRADITIONAL MUSIC AND SONG ASSOCIATION OF SCOTLAND

First published in Great Britain in 1995 by
Canongate Books Ltd, 14 High Street Edinburgh EH1 1TE

Copyright this collection © the Traditional Music and Song Association of Scotland
Individual tunes © as indicated

All rights reserved
The moral rights of the authors have been asserted

No part of this book may be reproduced or transmitted in any form or by
any means without written permission from the publisher, except by a reviewer
who wishes to quote brief passages in connection with a review written for
insertion in a magazine, newspaper or broadcast

Sponsored by United Distillers through its
Classic Malts of Scotland portfolio of single malt whiskies

CRAGGANMORE  DALWHINNIE
TALISKER   OBAN
GLENKINCHIE   LAGAVULIN

A United Distillers Sponsorship

The TMSA also acknowledge financial assistance from the Scottish Arts Council
towards the publication of this book

British Library Cataloguing-in-Publication Data
A catalogue record for this book is available upon request from the British Library

ISBN 0 86241 599 3

Typeset in Times and Petrucci by Andrew Thorburn
Printed and bound in Great Britain by
Cromwell Press, Broughton Gifford, Melksham, Wiltshire

Selected tunes from this collection are available on
CD and cassette from Greentrax Recordings

Foreword

Three hundred years ago, Martin Martin, whose book inspired Johnson's tour with Boswell, made numerous observations about the prevalence of musical ability and talent he encountered on his travels. In Lewis he noted that they *'are great lovers of music... they gave an account of eighteen men who could play on the violin pretty well without being taught.'* When he reached St. Kilda, he listened to a piper playing the notes of the gawlin fowl; he *'hath composed a tune of them, which the natives judge to be very fine music.'* Of his kinsfolk in Skye, Martin wrote:

> *They have a great genius for music and mechanics. I have observed several of their children that before they could speak were capable to distinguish and make the choice of one tune before another upon the violin... there are several of them who invent tunes very taking in the south of Scotland and elsewhere...*

Although there have been noteworthy musicians and composers in the intervening centuries, Scotland's music has travelled a rough, even threatening, path since Martin's day. Many of us have only dreamed of a time when we could find 'eighteen fiddlers' (or even one) in our community and we have too often been disheartened by premature obituaries for much-loved traditions.

As the twentieth century draws to a close, we see the blossoming and flourishing of Scottish traditional music and song. In no small way it is due to the concerted efforts and dedication of members and associates of the TMSA who have created opportunities for music-making that could never have happened outside the annual festivals and competitions. Each festival is different and, like whisky, some will be more to your taste than others.

How fitting it is to celebrate this 'great genius for music' - and mechanics, for that matter - with this collection of melodies composed in recent years by talented enthusiasts the length and breadth of the country. Warmest congratulations and thanks to the TMSA, to each individual - musicians, composers, producers, proofreaders and tea-makers - who contributed to *The Nineties Collection*, and to United Distillers whose generous sponsorship supported the project. Too many to name individually, Scotland can be proud of them all!

Margaret Bennett
School of Scottish Studies, Edinburgh

Introduction

In November 1990 the Traditional Music and Song Association of Scotland (TMSA) launched the 'Nineties Collection' Competition. The original idea for a collection of new compositions in the traditional idiom was conceived in the late eighties by musician Jim Sutherland who contacted TMSA's National Organiser at the time, Jane Fraser. With Texaco's financial input the competition went ahead to seek out the best of contemporary music in traditional style.

The response was staggering. Over 400 tunes poured in to the TMSA's office ranging from well-known names to musicians as young as eleven - clear indication that traditional playing and writing is alive and kicking! Judges for the awards, Aly Bain, Freeland Barbour, Hamish Henderson, Allan Macdonald, Robbie Shepherd and Savourna Stevenson met in Aberdeen in March 1991 to select the prizewinners in seven categories under the chairmanship of Jim Sutherland.

The excitement and enthusiasm generated by the competition moved the project into a higher gear. Ian Hardie - a notable fiddler and composer - was commissioned to edit the collection, combining the best of the competition entries with additional contributions from composers of note.

Through the generous sponsorship of the world's leading spirits company, United Distillers, and additional funding from the Scottish Arts Council, this book of over 200 tunes became a reality and was extended to include an accompanying CD and cassette on Greentrax Recordings.

The Nineties Collection is unique in representing the spread of new composition throughout the traditional music spectrum and, indeed, is the first time such a collection has been brought together in published form. As a milestone in Scottish traditional instrumental music it illustrates the range and quality of the idiom and its nineties interpretation in composition and performance.

The body of tunes in this book will be a resource for future generations of musicians and - well into the third millenium - a snapshot of composers and works current at the end of the 20th century. For reference or for enjoyment *The Nineties Collection* has something for all - fiddlers, pipers, accordionists, harpists - and under the umbrella of the Traditional Music and Song Association of Scotland encompasses the diversity of Scottish traditional music. The commitment, hard work and sheer enthusiasm of everyone involved in the Collection is a testament to the vigour of the Scottish musical tradition and the TMSA extends its thanks and appreciation to them all.

Lindsay Lewis, National Organiser
Traditional Music & Song Association of Scotland

Editorial Notes

The tunes in the collection are separated into tune type i.e. airs, strathspeys etc. and there is a chapter devoted wholly to pipe tunes of all types, which are shown with full settings. A miscellaneous chapter contains hornpipes, two-steps, polkas and a few tunes which are more difficult to categorise.

All non-pipe tunes have basic chord accompaniment symbols included, and these read above the stave and not below as common in some texts. Where not provided by the composer, these accompaniments have been arranged by Andy Thorburn, to whom many thanks. Bass notes have been omitted from the chord symbols but are taken as read in the flow of a normal accompaniment.

No ornamentation has been indicated (other than the pipe settings) and I believe that this is a matter for individual interpretation. The music on the page is simply the skeleton of the tune and the flesh is added only by the feeling and style provided by the individual musician. Similarly, the chord symbols are only intended as an easy guide and not as a definitive statement.

Tunes included which were entries in the 1991 competition are shown by these symbols:

+	winning entry
°	short-listed entry
*	unplaced entry

All other tunes are from invited composers.

The individual tune titles and headings include the area or town in which the composer lives, and these are shown as current at the time of publication or the 1991 competition. It is accepted that, as a consequence, some composers from distinctive native regional backgrounds will not feature as such.

The copyright dates shown beneath each tune are accurate insofar as known but, in a number of cases, are dated 1995 to coincide with the publication date of this collection or 1991 to coincide with the date of the original competition where full information is not available.

I should like to acknowledge the contributions made to this book by the following:
Andy Thorburn for typesetting, chord arrangements and general musical assistance;
Jim Sutherland as original competition editor;
Robbie Shepherd, Iain Macinnes, Freeland Barbour and **Jim Sutherland** for assistance in identifying composers;
Sheena Wellington and **Lindsay Lewis** of the Traditional Music and Song Association of Scotland for their varied input;
All composers for the opportunity to use their music;
George Bathgate and **Ken Robertson** of United Distillers for their assistance in enabling the publication of this book.

Ian Hardie
Nairn, 1995

Typesetting Notes

This is to establish and clarify the various conventions used in displaying music in print. The time signatures are standard and self-evident, with an occasional 2/4 instead of 4/4 or 2/2 reel. The key signatures follow three conventions - firstly, the standard music system of Western keys, from C to F# and back; secondly, the standard bagpipe notation of no indicated sharps or flats, the melody and ornaments written out in the key of A modal (some C naturals are included); thirdly, a combination of the two to indicate tunes in the modal pipe scale of A, with two sharps and a G natural.

Repeats are always indicated except for the forward repeat sign at the very start of the tune (the backward repeat is always given). A further convention used for alternative repeat bars is to show the second time music as notes in parentheses - this is used only where one or two notes are involved. The majority of tunes are set so that the musical parts start and finish at the end of a line for ease of reading; only where there are too many notes on one line does a repeat bar or double bar stand in the middle of a line.

Andy Thorburn
Evanton, 1995

THE NINETIES COLLECTION

Contents

Airs --- *page 1*

Hornpipes, Polkas and other tunes -------------------- *page 15*

Jigs -- *page 28*

Marches -- *page 44*

Pipe Tunes -- *page 60*

Reels -- *page 106*

Strathspeys -- *page 134*

Waltzes --- *page 144*

AIRS

Ambleside	Freeland Barbour	6
Balmashanner	Billy Jackson	2
Circle of Darkness	Phil Cunningham	4
Creag an Righ	Ian Hardie	12
Drinan	John Purser	5
Ellen Lynn Edward	Bob Edward	11
Elricks' Braes	Colin Dempster	8
Fornethy House	Peter Clark	9
Fuaran	Malcom Jones	14
Glen na Muice	Eric Allan	3
Grianachd	Malcolm Jones	12
Kveldsro	Ronnie Jamieson	11
Lament for Hector MacAndrew	Donald Goskirk	13
Marni Swanson of the Grey Coast	Andy Thorburn	8
Mistress Heywood's Fancy	Dougie Pincock	10
Mr. and Mrs. MacLean of Snaigow	Dougie MacLean	14
Mrs. Laura Taylor-Thoumire	Simon Thoumire	7
The Green Loch	Gary Coupland	2
The Grey Heron	Edith Clark	3
The Setting Sun	Ian Hardie	9
The Valley of Deeside	Hugh Melvin	4
Waltz Air	Eddie McGuire	5
Willie Fernie	Alasdair Fraser	7

CDI Track 4

The Green Loch

Gary Coupland
Edinburgh

© Gary Coupland 1995

Balmashanner

Billy Jackson
Forfar

© Billy Jackson 1995

The Grey Heron   +

Edith Clark
Edinburgh

© Edith Clark 1991

Glen na Muice °

Eric Allan
Inverness

© Eric Allan 1991

THE NINETIES COLLECTION

AIR No12

Circle of Darkness

Phil Cunningham

Beauly

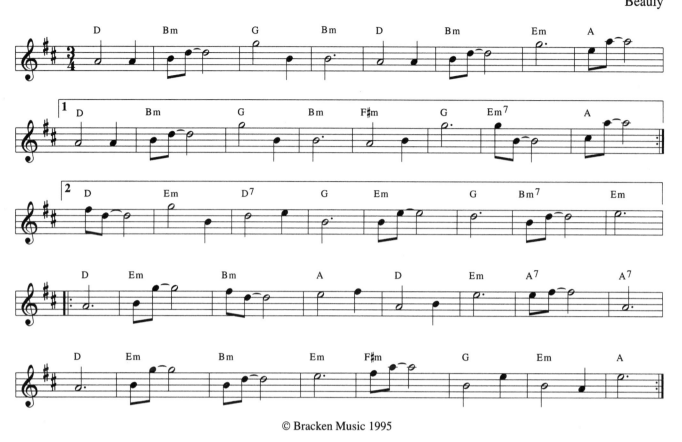

© Bracken Music 1995

AIR

The Valley of Deeside °

Hugh Melvin

Banchory

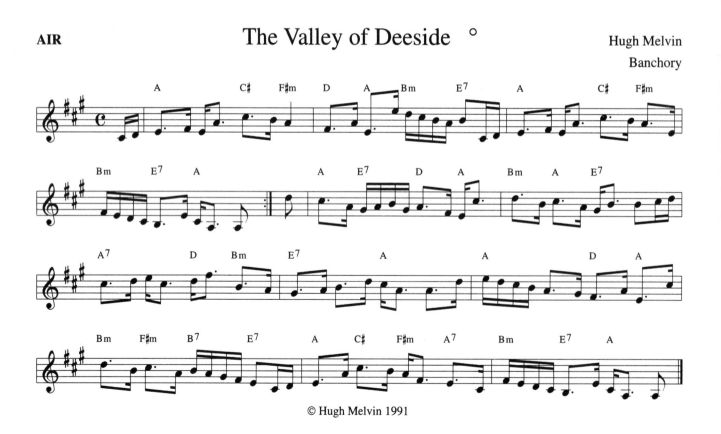

© Hugh Melvin 1991

Waltz Air

Eddie McGuire
Glasgow

© Eddie McGuire 1995

Drinan

John Purser
Glasgow

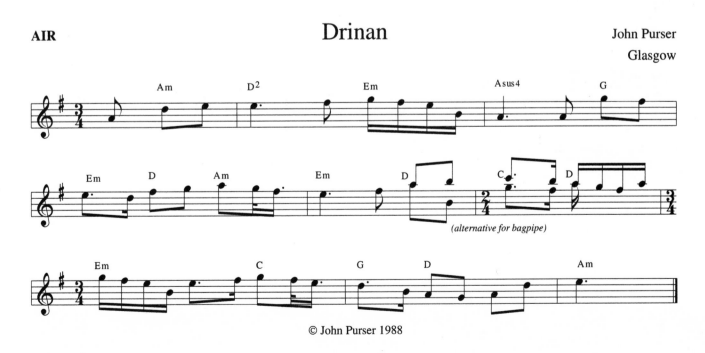

(alternative for bagpipe)

© John Purser 1988

THE NINETIES COLLECTION

AIR

Ambleside

Freeland Barbour
Edinburgh

© Bonskeid Music Ltd. 1995

AIR

Mrs. Laura Taylor-Thoumire

Simon Thoumire
Edinburgh

© Simon Thoumire 1995

AIR

Willie Fernie

Alasdair Fraser
California

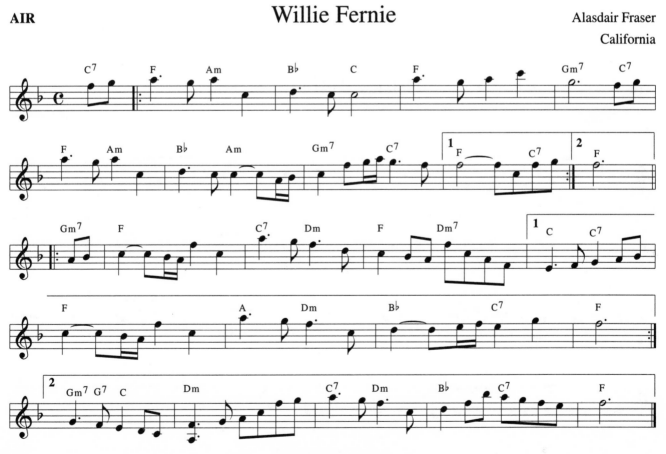

© Alasdair Fraser 1995

7

THE NINETIES COLLECTION

Marni Swanson of the Grey Coast

Andy Thorburn
Evanton

© Andy Thorburn 1995

Elricks' Braes *

Colin Dempster
Newmachar

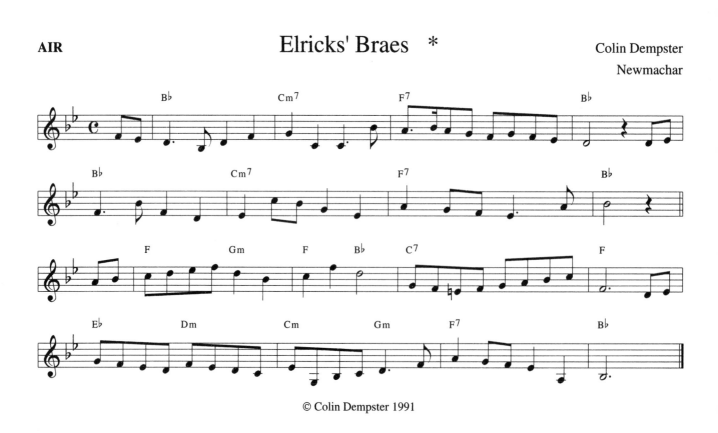

© Colin Dempster 1991

CD I TRACK 4

The Setting Sun

Ian Hardie
Nairn

© Ian Hardie 1995

Fornethy House

Peter Clark
Newton Stewart

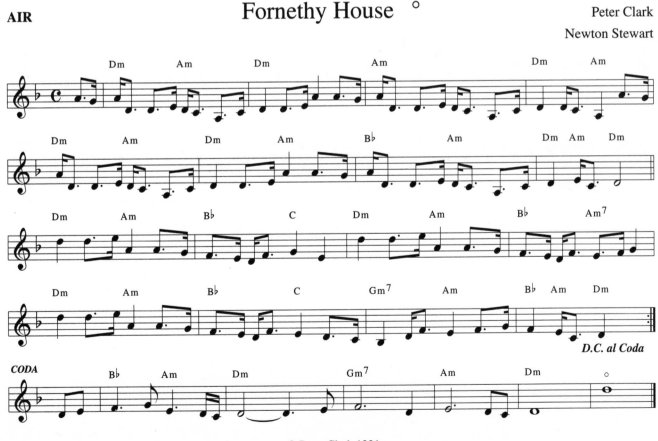

© Peter Clark 1991

9

Mistress Heywood's Fancy

Dougie Pincock
Dumbarton

© Grian Music 1993

Kveldsro °

Ronnie Jamieson
Shetland

© Ronnie Jamieson 1991

Ellen Lynn Edward *

Bob Edward
Dundee

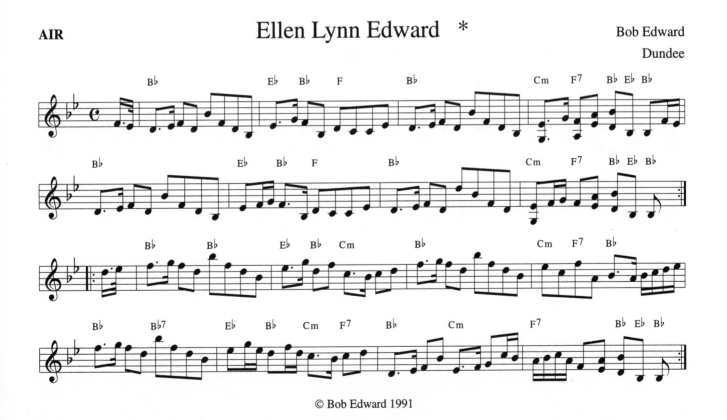

© Bob Edward 1991

THE NINETIES COLLECTION

Creag an Righ

Ian Hardie
Nairn

© Ian Hardie 1993

Grianachd

Malcolm Jones
Edinburgh

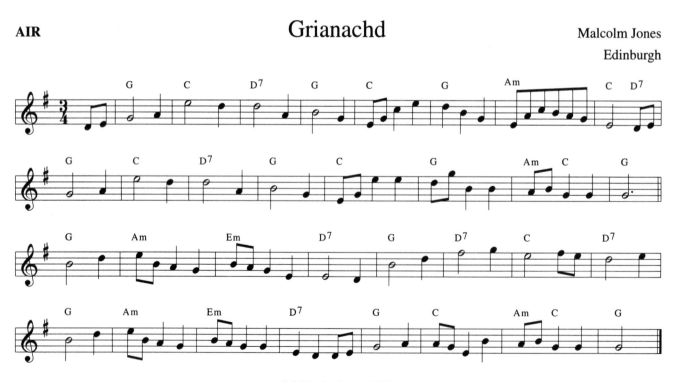

© Malcolm Jones 1995

AIR

Lament for Hector MacAndrew

Donald Goskirk
Dornoch

© Donald Goskirk 1995

Fuaran

Malcolm Jones
Edinburgh

© Malcolm Jones 1995

Mr and Mrs MacLean of Snaigow

Dougie MacLean
Dunkeld

© Limetree Arts and Music 1984

HORNPIPES, POLKAS and OTHER TUNES

HORNPIPES

Clark's Cases --------------------------------- Gary Peterson -------------------------- 25
Da Bouster Boy--------------------------------- Debbie Scott---------------------------- 24
Father Tom ------------------------------------- Davy Tulloch--------------------------- 26
△Paul Anderson's Hornpipe --------------------- George Carmichael--------------------- 25
△St. Gilbert's Hornpipe ------------------------- Eric Allan ------------------------------ 24
△The Marianna --------------------------------- Bill Cook ------------------------------- 27

POLKAS

The Grace Renwick Polka ---------------------- Iain MacPhail -------------------------- 22
The Iris Lawrie Polka--------------------------- Ian Crichton --------------------------- 23

TWO-STEPS

The Doune Lodge Two-Step -------------------- Iain Peterson -------------------------- 19
The Jimmy Burgess Two-Step ----------------- Iain MacPhail -------------------------- 20
The Lilt o' Stanley ----------------------------- Bert Murray ---------------------------- 21

Danielle's Dance ------------------------------- Eddie McGuire------------------------- 17
Fish Feis --------------------------------------- Wendy Stewart------------------------- 16
Nan of the Strath ------------------------------- Addie Harper --------------------------- 17
Planxty Crockery ------------------------------ Patsy Seddon -------------------------- 16
✕The Gael -------------------------------------- Dougie MacLean ---------------------- 18

✕ CDI Track 1
△ CDI Track 2

HARP TUNE

Planxty Crockery

Patsy Seddon
Edinburgh

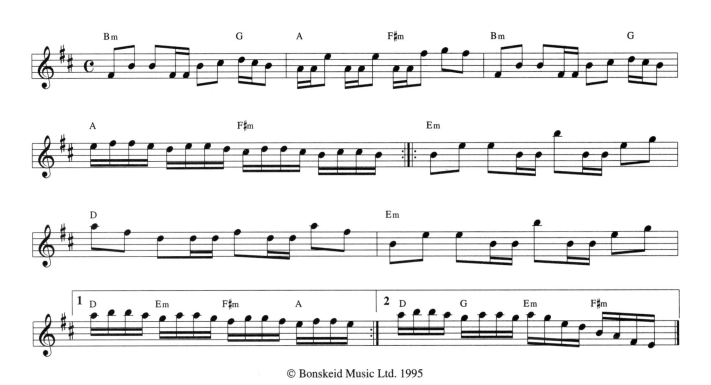

© Bonskeid Music Ltd. 1995

HARP TUNE

Fish Feis

Wendy Stewart
Edinburgh

(last time only)

© Wendy Stewart 1995

STRATHSPEY AIR

Danielle's Dance

Eddie McGuire
Glasgow

© Eddie McGuire 1994   *(original key Eb)*

BARN DANCE

Nan of the Strath

Addie Harper
Wick

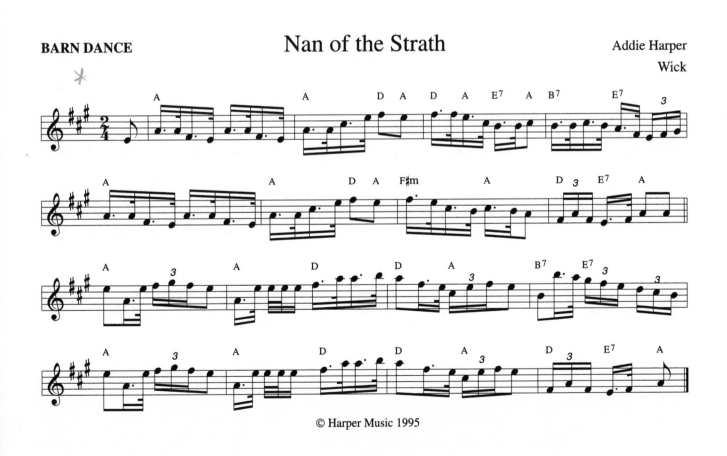

© Harper Music 1995

The Gael

Dougie MacLean
Dunkeld

AIR

JIG

© Limetree Arts and Music 1990

TWO-STEP

The Doune Lodge Two-Step

Iain Peterson
Dollar

FINE

D.C. al Fine

© Shian Music 1995

THE NINETIES COLLECTION

The Jimmy Burgess Two-Step

Iain MacPhail
Edinburgh

2nd time to next line
3rd time to TRIO

FINE

last time

2nd time D.S. al Trio

TRIO

2nd time D.S. al Fine

© Iain MacPhail 1995

The Lilt o' Stanley

TWO STEP

Bert Murray
Aberdeen

2nd time go to next line
3rd time go to Trio

D.C. al Trio

TRIO

© Bert Murray 1995

POLKA

The Grace Renwick Polka

Iain MacPhail
Edinburgh

© Iain MacPhail 1995

The Iris Laurie Polka

Ian Crichton
Stornoway

© Rowancroft Music 1994

CDI Track 2

St Gilbert's Hornpipe *

Eric Allan
Inverness

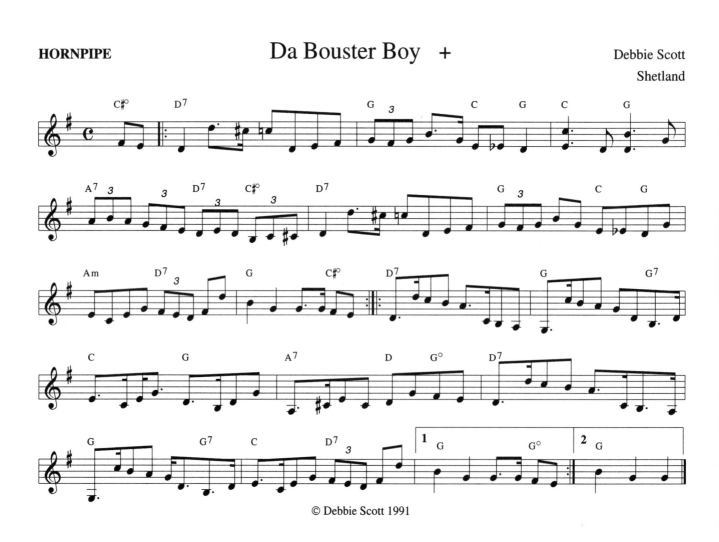

© Eric Allan 1991

HORNPIPE

Da Bouster Boy +

Debbie Scott
Shetland

© Debbie Scott 1991

CDI Track 2

HORNPIPE

Paul Anderson's Hornpipe

George Carmichael
Dundee

© Ancrum Music 1994

HORNPIPE

Clark's Cases

Gary Peterson
Shetland

© Gary Peterson 1995

THE NINETIES COLLECTION

HORNPIPE

Father Tom

Davy Tulloch

Ayr

© Davy Tulloch 1995

CDI Track2

HORNPIPE

The Marianna °

Bill Cook

Clackmannan

2nd time go to next line
3rd time go to 𝄋

D.C. al Segno

© Bill Cook 1991

27

JIGS

Amy's Rollerskates ---------------------------- Mary Macmaster ----------------------- 32
Amy's Tune ------------------------------------- George Carmichael --------------------- 34
Becky Taylor's Audacity ---------------------- Simon Thoumire ----------------------- 35
✳ Crabbit Shona (The Remix) ------------------- Angus R. Grant ------------------------- 30
✳ Discovery ------------------------------------ Mary Ann Kennedy -------------------- 37
✳ Dun Ibrig ------------------------------------- Dr. John Holliday --------------------- 39
Jig of the Clan Beag --------------------------- Andy Thorburn ------------------------ 39
John Sinclair Younger of Ulbster -------------- Addie Harper ------------------------- 31
Maureen's Jig ---------------------------------- Fergie Macdonald --------------------- 40
The Prize -- Sandy Mathers ------------------------- 36
One Hundred Years of Sailing ----------------- Steven Spence ------------------------- 33
Miss Patricia Simpson's Jig -------------------- John Renton --------------------------- 32
North Turned South ---------------------------- Dr. John Holliday --------------------- 40
Polly Rhythm ----------------------------------- Martyn Bennett ----------------------- 38
Snoogles' Jig ----------------------------------- Martyn Bennett ----------------------- 41
⌂ The Road to Banff ----------------------------- Malcolm Reavell ---------------------- 31
The Clay Pigeon Boxer ------------------------- Ian Crichton -------------------------- 33
The Deserts of Harthill ------------------------- Sandy Harvey ------------------------- 29
The Dingwall Jig ------------------------------- David Gordon ------------------------- 42
The Jig Runrig --------------------------------- Fergie Macdonald --------------------- 43
✳ The Point Road -------------------------------- Iain Macleod ------------------------- 34
✳ The Streams of Abernethy --------------------- Wendy Stewart ------------------------ 30
The Stroopie Brae ------------------------------ Ian Duncan --------------------------- 35
The Wee Twister ------------------------------- David Gordon ------------------------- 43
Under a Northern Sky -------------------------- Andy Thorburn ------------------------ 36
Willie Gillingham, R. M. ----------------------- Muriel Johnstone --------------------- 29

✳ CD1 Track 10
⌂ no CD track

JIG

The Deserts of Harthill °

Sandy Harvey
Camelon

© Sandy Harvey 1991

JIG

Willie Gillingham R.M.

Muriel Johnstone
Duns

© Scotscores 1993

29

THE NINETIES COLLECTION

CD I
No 10

(3.05)

JIG

The Streams of Abernethy

Wendy Stewart
Edinburgh

© Grian Music 1992

CD I No 10 (3.35) → (4.35)

JIG

Crabbit Shona (The Remix)

Angus R. Grant
Edinburgh

© Angus R. Grant 1995

D.S. al Fine

The Road to Banff *

Malcolm Reavell
Newmachar

© Malcolm Reavell 1991

John Sinclair Younger of Ulbster

Addie Harper
Wick

© Harper Music 1993

Amy's Rollerskates

Mary Macmaster
Edinburgh

© Bonskeid Music Ltd. 1991

Miss Patricia Simpson's Jig

John Renton
Inveraray

© John Renton 1995

32

no CD

JIG

100 Years of Sailing

Steven Spence
Shetland

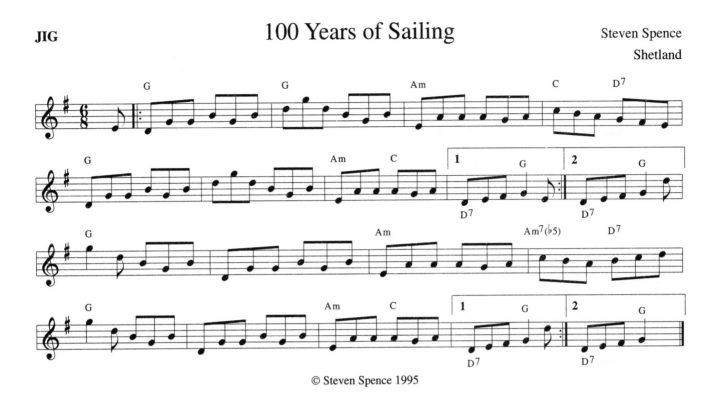

© Steven Spence 1995

JIG

The Clay Pigeon Boxer
(Fergie Macdonald's Jig)

Ian Crichton
Stornoway

© Rowancroft Music 1993

THE NINETIES COLLECTION

JIG

Amy's Tune

George Carmichael
Dundee

© Ancrum Music 1994

JIG

The Point Road

Iain Macleod
Edinburgh

© Grian Music 1994

34

JIG

Becky Taylor's Audacity

Simon Thoumire
Edinburgh

© Simon Thoumire 1995

JIG

The Stroopie Brae

Ian Duncan
Keith

© Ian Duncan 1995

THE NINETIES COLLECTION

The Prize - or
Michael Easton's Jig °

Sandy Mathers
Auchtermuchty

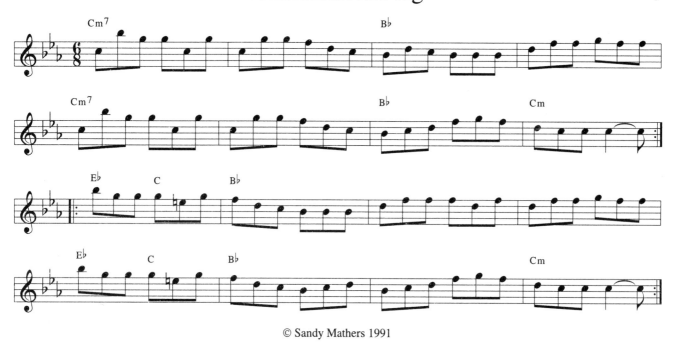

© Sandy Mathers 1991

JIG

Under A Northern Sky

Andy Thorburn
Evanton

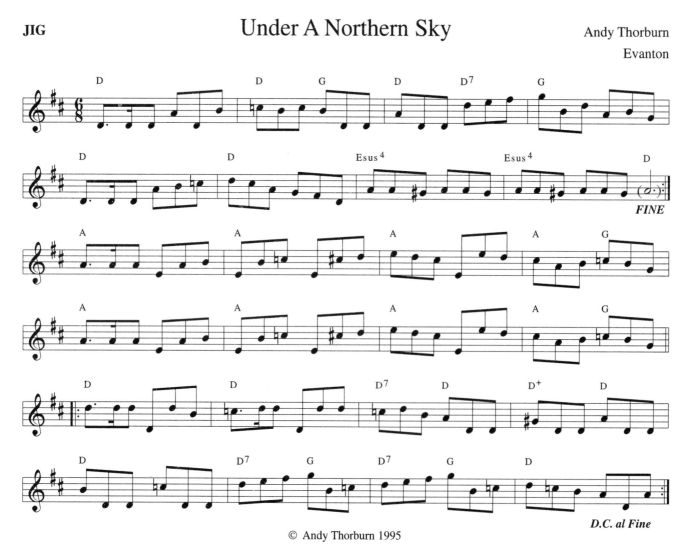

FINE

D.C. al Fine

© Andy Thorburn 1995

(0.00)

JIG

Discovery °

Mary Ann Kennedy
Inverness

© Mary Ann Kennedy 1991

THE NINETIES COLLECTION

JIG

Polly Rhythm

Martyn Bennett
Edinburgh

© Martyn Bennett 1995

CDI No.10
(1.00)

JIG

Dun Ibrig °

Dr. John Holliday
Tiree

© Dr. John Holliday 1991

JIG

Jig of the Clan Beag

Andy Thorburn
Evanton

© Andy Thorburn 1995

North Turned South +

Dr John Holliday

Tiree

© Dr. John Holliday 1991

Maureen's Jig

Fergie Macdonald

Acharacle

© Fergie Macdonald 1995

Snoogles' Jig

Martyn Bennett
Edinburgh

© Martyn Bennett 1995

The Dingwall Jig

David Gordon
Invergordon

Variation 1

Variation 2

Variation 3

© David Gordon 1991

The Wee Twister

David Gordon
Invergordon

© David Gordon 1995

The Jig Runrig

Fergie Macdonald
Acharacle

Play this tune 4 times through, first in D, then in key
G, key A and finally back to D

© Fergie Macdonald 1995

MARCHES

2/4

Campbell's Heels -- Freeland Barbour ------ 50
Iain MacPhail's Compliments to the late Chrissie Leatham ----------- Iain MacPhail ---------- 53
John Crawford's March --- Colin Dewar ----------- 47
John Florence of Monymusk --- Jim Emslie ------------- 45
Ronald M. Dallas-- John Dallas ------------ 48
The Dance of the Roag Salmon --------------------------------------- Phil Cunningham ------ 46
The Falcon -- Gordon Pattullo ------- 49
The Fiddlers' Welcome --- Norman Kerr ---------- 51
Torbeag --- Gordon Pattullo ------- 54
Welcome to Ballindalloch Castle ------------------------------------- Ian Duncan ------------ 52

4/4

Anda Campbell's March -- Colin Dewar ----------- 51
Augusta --- Charlie Soane --------- 47
Julie and James Rollo's Wedding March ------------------------------ Addie Harper---------- 59
Mrs. Meddles' March--- Simon Thoumire ------ 49
Mrs. Meg Jamieson of Roadside Cottage ----------------------------- Ronnie Jamieson ------ 45
Sandy Fenton's --- Freeland Barbour ------ 56
The Bicentennial March-- Bert Murray ----------- 55

6/8

Gibbie's Ceilidh -- Ian Duncan ------------ 58
A March for Morven May -- Addie Harper---------- 57

MARCH

Mrs. Meg Jamieson of Roadside Cottage °

Ronnie Jamieson
Shetland

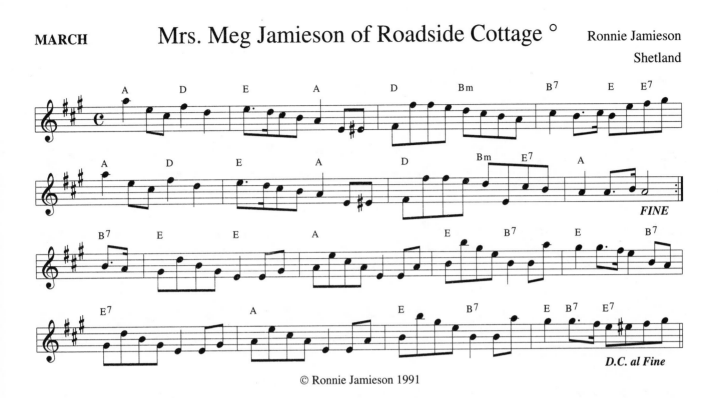

© Ronnie Jamieson 1991

MARCH

John Florence of Monymusk °

Jim Emslie
Inverurie

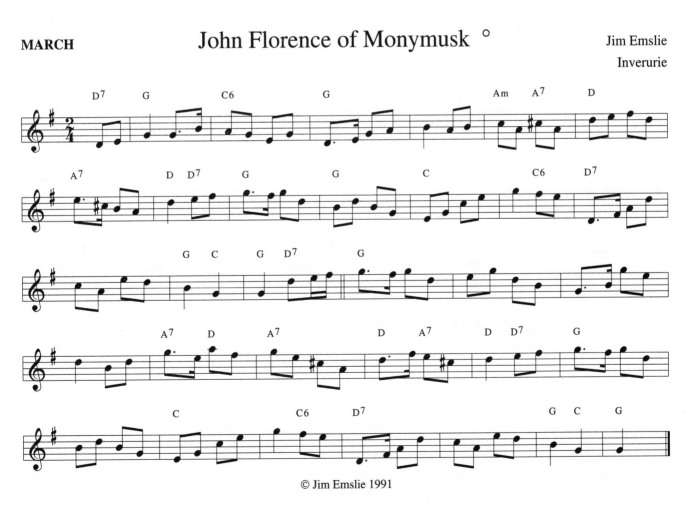

© Jim Emslie 1991

MARCH

The Dance of the Roag Salmon

Phil Cunningham

Beauly

© Bracken Music 1995

Augusta   *

Charlie Soane
Glasgow

© Charlie Soane 1991

John Crawford's March

Colin Dewar
Freuchie

© Bonskeid Music Ltd. 1994

THE NINETIES COLLECTION

MARCH

Ronald M. Dallas +

John Dallas
Falkirk

© John Dallas 1991

Mrs. Meddles' March

Simon Thoumire
Edinburgh

© Simon Thoumire 1995

The Falcon

Gordon Pattullo
Coupar Angus

© Sunshine Music 1995

MARCH

Campbell's Heels

Freeland Barbour
Edinburgh

© Bonskeid Music Ltd. 1995

Anda Campbell's March

Colin Dewar
Freuchie

© Bonskeid Music Ltd. 1987

The Fiddlers' Welcome °

Norman Kerr
Glasgow

© Norman Kerr 1991

THE NINETIES COLLECTION

Welcome to Ballindalloch Castle

Ian Duncan
Keith

© Ian Duncan 1995

MARCH

Iain MacPhail's Compliments
to the Late Chrissie Leatham

Iain MacPhail
Edinburgh

© Iain MacPhail 1995

MARCH

Torbeag

Gordon Pattullo
Coupar Angus

© Sunshine Music 1995

The Bicentennial March
Union Street, Aberdeen

Bert Murray
Aberdeen

© Bert Murray 1995

THE NINETIES COLLECTION

Sandy Fenton's

Freeland Barbour
Edinburgh

© Bonskeid Music Ltd. 1995

A March for Morven May

Addie Harper

Wick

© Harper Music 1995

THE NINETIES COLLECTION

MARCH

Gibbie's Ceilidh

Ian Duncan
Keith

© Ian Duncan 1995

Julie and James Rollo's Wedding March

Addie Harper

Wick

© Harper Music 1995

PIPE TUNES

AIRS

Loch Flemington --- Wm. M. MacDonald ------------ 75
Round Dawn -- Hamish Moore ------------------- 95
Song for Chris --- Dougie Pincock ------------------ 63
The White Water -- George Macilwham ------------- 78

HORNPIPES

College of Piping - "Summerside" P.E.I. ----------------------- Roderick S. Macdonald --------- 93
Tanks for the Memories --- Dougie Pincock ------------------ 91
The Barlinnie Highlander --------------------------------------- Robert Wallace ------------------ 89
The Jaffa Club --- Jim Wark ------------------------ 78
The Passive Drinker --- Roderick S. MacDonald -------- 97

JIGS

2nd at Pugwash -- Roderick S. MacDonald -------- 83
Dr. Iain MacAonghais --- Allan Macdonald ---------------- 85
Kevin Barry of Nigg --- Duncan MacGillivray ----------- 96
Roll Out the Snake -- Gordon Duncan ------------------ 95
The Loon wi' the Stripped Sark --------------------------------- Ian Sutherland ------------------- 99
The Parks of Kenway -- Duncan MacGillivray ----------- 86

QUICKSTEP

The Road to Loch nam Bearneas -------------------------------- Allan Macdonald ---------------- 81

2/4 MARCHES

Balnauld Cottage -- Gordon Duncan ---------------- 101
Donald Archie Macdonald -------------------------------------- Allan Macdonald ---------------- 64
Ezekiel Sturgeon -- Angus Lawrie -------------------- 66
Father Roddy MacAulay's Welcome to Oban ------------------- Duncan Johnstone --------------- 68
Inverness British Legion -- Evan Gair ------------------------ 70
John Kerr's Jacket --- Donald MacPherson ------------- 72
Mrs. Doreen Lawrie -- Angus Lawrie ------------------ 104
Sir James of the Bings -- Gordon Duncan ------------------ 74
The Argyllshire Gathering's Welcome to Its Gold Medal ------- Allan Macdonald ---------------- 62
The Stormyhill Gathering --------------------------------------- Malcolm Jones ------------------- 76
Trevisans' March -- Donald MacPherson ------------ 79

PIPE TUNES (continued)

6/8 MARCHES

Ann Marie Campbell's March ---------------------------------- Duncan Johnstone ---------------- 80
Dr. Jimmy Campbell's Welcome Home -------------------------- Duncan Johnstone -------------- 105
General Eisenhower's Welcome at Culzean Castle -------------- George Macilwham -------------- 82
Saorsa --- Duncan Johnstone ---------------- 84
Stephen Cooper -- Roderick S. MacDonald --------- 88
The Booths of Comrie --- Donald MacPherson ----------- 103
The Gairs of Delny House ------------------------------------- Evan Gair ------------------------ 90
The Trees of North Uist --------------------------------------- Wm. M. MacDonald ----------- 102
Tom Macgregor -- Duncan MacGillivray ----------- 92

9/8 MARCH

◯Tianavaig -- Dr. Angus Macdonald ----------- 94

REELS

Break Yer Bass Drone --- Gordon Duncan ------------------- 65
Dance of the Woodbug -- Dr. Angus Macdonald ----------- 77
Farewell to Decorum -- Hamish Moore ------------------- 75
Maggie's Reel -- Hamish Moore ------------------- 69
Sheep Running About -- Martyn Bennett ------------------- 73
The Corby Candle --- Frances O'Rourke --------------- 98

RETREAT

Farewell to Muirheads -- Robert Wallace ------------------- 71

STRATHSPEYS

◯Betty Jessiman -- Wm. M. MacDonald ------------- 69
Dun Mhuirrich -- George Macilwham ------------ 100
Duncan Johnstone's Strathspey ------------------------------- Robert Wallace ------------------- 67
Laurie McKillop --- Jim Wark ------------------------- 87
Port Allan O'g -- Dr. Angus Macdonald ----------- 98

WALTZ

Sarah's Waltz -- Angus Lawrie -------------------- 63

◯ CD I Track 3

MARCH

The Argyllshire Gathering's
Welcome to Its Gold Medal

Allan Macdonald
Edinburgh

© Allan Macdonald 1995

Sarah's Waltz

Angus Lawrie
Largs

© Angus Lawrie 1995

Song for Chris

Dougie Pincock
Dumbarton

© Grian Music 1994

MARCH

Donald Archie MacDonald

Allan Macdonald
Edinburgh

© Allan Macdonald 1995

REEL

Break Yer Bass Drone

Gordon Duncan
Pitlochry

© Grian Music 1994

MARCH

Ezekiel Sturgeon

Angus Lawrie
Largs

© Angus Lawrie 1995

STRATHSPEY

Duncan Johnstone's Strathspey

Robert Wallace
Glasgow

© Scottish Music Publishing 1986
(Scottish Music Information Centre)

THE NINETIES COLLECTION

Fr. Roddy MacAulay's
Welcome to Oban

Duncan Johnstone
Glasgow

© Duncan Johnstone 1995

68

Betty Jessiman

Wm. M. MacDonald
Inverness

© Wm. M. MacDonald 1995

REEL

Maggie's Reel

Hamish Moore
Birnam

© Hamish Moore 1993

Inverness British Legion °

Evan Gair
Inverness

© Shian Music 1995

Farewell to Muirheads

Robert Wallace
Glasgow

© Scottish Music Publishing 1986
(Scottish Music Information Centre)

John Kerr's Jacket

Donald MacPherson
Balbeggie

© Donald MacPherson 1995

REEL

Sheep Running About

Martyn Bennett
Edinburgh

© Martyn Bennett 1995

MARCH

Sir James of the Bings

Gordon Duncan
Pitlochry

© Gordon Duncan 1995

REEL

Farewell to Decorum

Hamish Moore
Birnam

© Grian Music 1993

AIR

Loch Flemington

Wm. M. MacDonald
Inverness

© Wm. M. MacDonald 1995

THE NINETIES COLLECTION

The Stormyhill Gathering

Malcolm Jones
Edinburgh

© Malcolm Jones 1995

REEL

Dance of the Woodbug

Dr. Angus Macdonald
Portree

© Dr. Angus Macdonald 1995

The White Water

George Macilwham
Glasgow

© George Macilwham 1995

The Jaffa Club

Jim Wark
Glasgow

repeat 2nd time 2nd part

© Jim Wark 1995

MARCH

Trevisans' March

Donald MacPherson
Balbeggie

© Donald MacPherson 1992

THE NINETIES COLLECTION

Ann Marie Campbell's March

Duncan Johnstone
Glasgow

© Duncan Johnstone 1995

QUICKSTEP

The Road to Loch nam Bearneas

Allan Macdonald
Edinburgh

© Allan Macdonald 1995

THE NINETIES COLLECTION

General Eisenhower's Welcome
at Culzean Castle

George Macilwham

Glasgow

© George Macilwham 1990

JIG

2nd at Pugwash

Roderick S. MacDonald
London

© Roderick S. MacDonald 1995

THE NINETIES COLLECTION

MARCH

Saorsa

Duncan Johnstone
Glasgow

© Duncan Johnstone 1995

JIG

Dr. Iain MacAonghais

Allan Macdonald
Edinburgh

© Allan Macdonald 1995

JIG

The Parks of Kenway

Duncan MacGillivray
Tain

© Duncan MacGillivray 1995

The Parks of Kenway (continued)

© Duncan MacGillivray 1995

STRATHSPEY

Laurie McKillop

Jim Wark
Glasgow

© Jim Wark 1995

MARCH

Stephen Cooper

Roderick S. MacDonald
London

© Roderick S. MacDonald 1995

HORNPIPE

The Barlinnie Highlander

Robert Wallace
Glasgow

© Scottish Music Publishing 1986
(Scottish Music Information Centre)

THE NINETIES COLLECTION

The Gairs of Delny House °

Evan Gair
Inverness

© Shian Music 1991

Tanks for the Memories

Dougie Pincock
Dumbarton

© Grian Music 1994

MARCH

Tom Macgregor

Duncan MacGillivray
Tain

© Duncan MacGillivray 1995

HORNPIPE

The College of Piping -
"Summerside", P.E.I.

Roderick S. MacDonald
London

© Roderick S. MacDonald 1995

THE NINETIES COLLECTION

MARCH

Tianavaig

Dr. Angus Macdonald
Portree

© Dr. Angus Macdonald 1995

Roll Out The Snake *

JIG

Gordon Duncan
Pitlochry

© Gordon Duncan 1991

Round Dawn

AIR

Hamish Moore
Birnam

© Hamish Moore 1993

Kevin Barry of Nigg

Duncan MacGillivray
Tain

© Duncan MacGillivray 1995

HORNPIPE

The Passive Drinker

Roderick S. MacDonald
London

© Roderick S. MacDonald 1995

THE NINETIES COLLECTION

The Corby Candle °

Frances O'Rourke
Corby

© Frances O'Rourke 1991

Port Allan O'g

Dr. Angus Macdonald
Portree

© Kinmor Music 1995

The Loon wi' the Stripped Sark +

Ian Sutherland
Aberdeen

© Ian Sutherland 1991

THE NINETIES COLLECTION

STRATHSPEY

Dun Mhuirrich

George Macilwham
Glasgow

© George Macilwham 1995

MARCH

Balnauld Cottage °

Gordon Duncan
Pitlochry

© Gordon Duncan 1991

THE NINETIES COLLECTION

MARCH

The Trees of North Uist

Wm. M. MacDonald
Inverness

© Wm. M. MacDonald 1995

MARCH

The Booths of Comrie

Donald MacPherson
Balbeggie

© Donald MacPherson 1995

MARCH

Mrs. Doreen Lawrie

Angus Lawrie
Largs

© Angus Lawrie 1995

Dr. Jimmy Campbell's Welcome Home

MARCH

Duncan Johnstone
Glasgow

© Duncan Johnstone 1995

REELS

Alasdair Fraser's Compliments to Lorna Mitchell --------- Alasdair Fraser ----------- 107
Ally Kerr -- Jim Ramsay ------------- 116
△Andy Broon's Reel --------------------------------------- Aly Bain ----------------- 108
Annie Lawson --- Brian McNeill ----------- 126
Assynt Crofters -- Brian McNeill ----------- 123
Bert ' Mega' Murray -------------------------------------- Karen Steven ------------- 119
Bob McQuillin's Reel ------------------------------------- Aly Bain ----------------- 131
Bogey Broke the Back Door -------------------------------- Ronnie Jamieson ------- 131
Bunji's Dilemma -- Charlie Soane ----------- 113
Clancy's Salsa --- George Carmichael ----- 121
Clifton Reel --- Marianne Burns --------- 115
Da Eye Wifie --- Iain Macleod ------------- 126
Dad's Tune --- Ian Lowthian ------------- 119
Dave Jackson's Reel -------------------------------------- Davy Tulloch ------------ 123
△Debbie Ann's Reel --------------------------------------- Ronnie Jamieson ------- 110
Eoghainn Iain Alasdair B.E.M. --------------------------- Dr. John Holliday ------- 109
Hair in the Gate --- Jim Sutherland ---------- 109
In Memory of John Pottinger ------------------------------ Davy Tulloch ------------ 120
△Jocky's Treble Tops ------------------------------------- Brian McNeill ----------- 108
Leith Central -- Gary Coupland ---------- 118
Living by the Sea -- Jim Sutherland ---------- 125
Peats in Skow -- Karen Steven ------------- 132
Phil Cunningham's Reel ----------------------------------- Aly Bain ----------------- 127
Pinewoods Auction -- Muriel Johnstone -------- 116
Pushing the Porsche -------------------------------------- Patsy Seddon ------------- 127

△ CD Track 1
Ⅰ

REELS (continued)

Rayburn Reel ---------------------------------- Steven Spence ------------------------ 113

Reel for Eilidh Shaw ---------------------------- Russell Hunter ------------------------ 125

Skye Barbecue --------------------------------- Alasdair Fraser ------------------------ 120

Starjump -------------------------------------- Simon Thoumire ---------------------- 111

T. C. Humbley's ------------------------------- Angus R. Grant ----------------------- 128

The Christening Piece --------------------------- Stuart Eydmann ----------------------- 128

The Doon-Hingin' Tie --------------------------- Iain Peterson ------------------------- 118

The Fiddle Cushion ---------------------------- Simon Bradley ----------------------- 124

The Flawless Juggler --------------------------- Mary Macmaster --------------------- 122

The Forfar Reel -------------------------------- Billy Jackson ------------------------- 121

The Fyrish Reel -------------------------------- David Gordon ------------------------ 122

The Laggan Stockman -------------------------- Gordon Pattullo ---------------------- 130

The Men from Inveraray ------------------------ Ian Crichton ------------------------- 117

The Ness Lassies' Reel ------------------------- Phil Cunningham -------------------- 110

The Open Fence -------------------------------- Ian Hardie -------------------------- 114

The Osprey in the Bay -------------------------- Adrian Ledingham ------------------- 111

The Reunion Reel ------------------------------ Fergie Macdonald ------------------- 114

The Salvation ---------------------------------- Simon Bradley ---------------------- 130

The Wan-Legged Yow -------------------------- Thomas Mainland ------------------- 112

The Willowbank Reel -------------------------- Peter Brash ------------------------- 117

Tossing the Mane ------------------------------ Patsy Seddon ------------------------ 107

William John More ----------------------------- Davy Tulloch ------------------------ 129

The Witches of Mull --------------------------- Eddie McGuire ----------------------- 132

CD I
No 5

Alasdair Fraser's Compliments to Lorna Mitchell

REEL

Alasdair Fraser
California

© Alasdair Fraser 1995

Tossing the Mane

REEL

Patsy Seddon
Edinburgh

© Patsy Seddon 1995

CD I ... Hol

REEL

Andy Broon's Reel

Aly Bain
Edinburgh

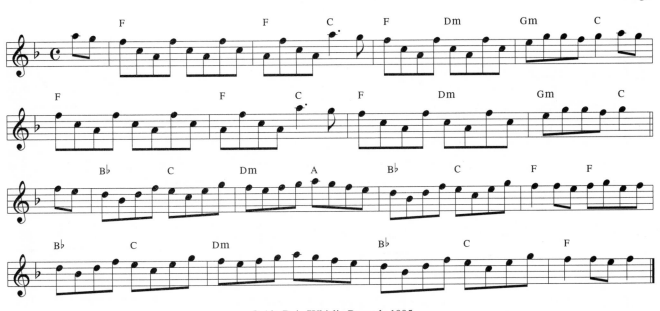

© Aly Bain/Whirlie Records 1995

CD I Track 1

REEL

Jocky's Treble Tops

Brian McNeill
County Durham

© Brian McNeill 1995

THE NINETIES COLLECTION

REEL

Eoghainn Iain Alasdair, B.E.M. °

Dr. John Holliday
Tiree

© Dr. John Holliday 1991

REEL

Hair in the Gate

Jim Sutherland
Edinburgh

© Jim Sutherland 1995

REEL

The Ness Lassies Reel

Phil Cunningham

Beauly

© Bracken Music 1995

REEL

Debbie Ann's Reel *

Ronnie Jamieson

Shetland

© Ronnie Jamieson 1991

THE NINETIES COLLECTION

Starjump

Simon Thoumire
Edinburgh

© Simon Thoumire 1993

The Osprey in the Bay °

Adrian Ledingham
Aberdeen

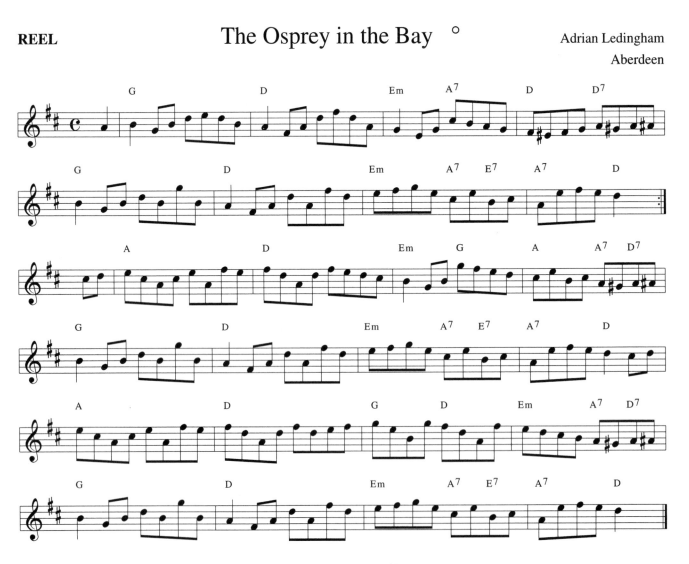

© Adrian Ledingham 1991

The Wan-Legged Yow +

Thomas Mainland
Orkney

© Thomas Mainland 1991

THE NINETIES COLLECTION

Rayburn Reel

Steven Spence
Shetland

© Steven Spence 1995

Bunji's Dilemma

Charlie Soane
Glasgow

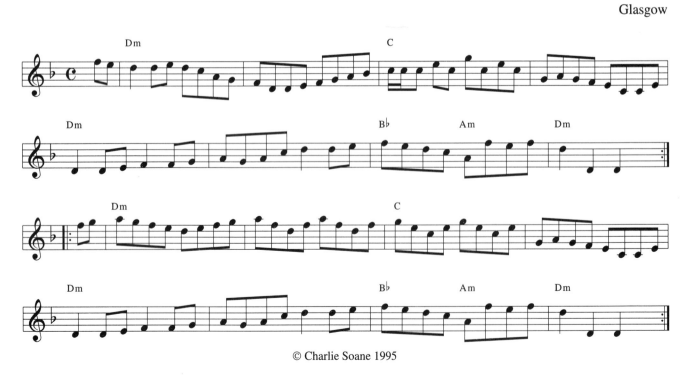

© Charlie Soane 1995

The Open Fence

Ian Hardie
Nairn

© Ian Hardie 1995

The Reunion Reel

Fergie Macdonald
Acharacle

© Fergie Macdonald 1995

THE NINETIES COLLECTION

Clifton Reel °

Marianne Burns
Aberdeen

© Marianne Burns 1991

116

Ally Kerr °

Jim Ramsay

Arbroath

© Jim Ramsay 1991

Pinewoods Auction

Muriel Johnstone

Duns

© Scotscores 1989

THE NINETIES COLLECTION

The Men from Inveraray

Ian Crichton
Stornoway

© Rowancroft Music 1993

The Willowbank Reel °

Peter Brash
Edinburgh

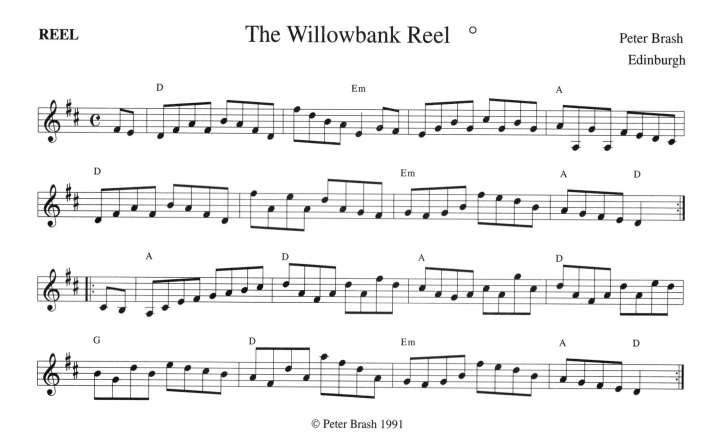

© Peter Brash 1991

REEL

Leith Central

Gary Coupland
Edinburgh

© Gary Coupland 1995

REEL

The Doon-Hingin' Tie

Iain Peterson
Dollar

© Shian Music 1995

THE NINETIES COLLECTION

REEL

Dad's Tune *

Ian Lowthian
Harrow

© Ian Lowthian 1991

REEL

Bert 'Mega' Murray *

Karen Steven
Wick

© Karen Steven 1991

Skye Barbecue

Alasdair Fraser
California

© Alasdair Fraser 1995

In memory of John Pottinger

Davy Tulloch
Ayr

© Davy Tulloch 1995

THE NINETIES COLLECTION

The Forfar Reel

Billy Jackson

Forfar

© Billy Jackson 1995

Clancy's Salsa

George Carmichael

Dundee

© Ancrum Music 1994

The Fyrish Reel

David Gordon
Invergordon

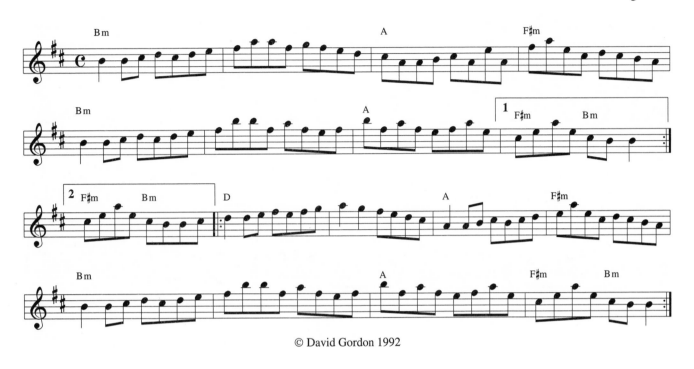

© David Gordon 1992

The Flawless Juggler

Mary Macmaster
Edinburgh

© Bonskeid Music Ltd. 1991

Assynt Crofters

Brian McNeill
County Durham

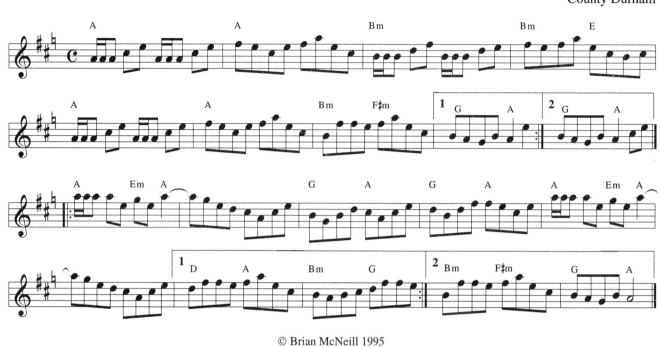

© Brian McNeill 1995

Dave Jackson's Reel

Davy Tulloch
Ayr

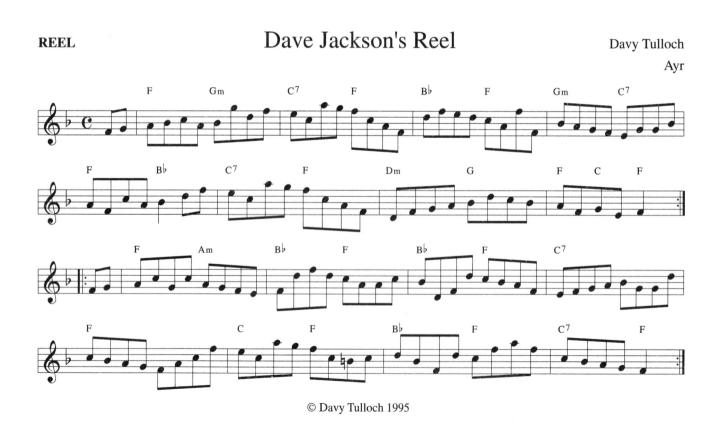

© Davy Tulloch 1995

The Fiddle Cushion

Simon Bradley
Edinburgh

© Simon Bradley 1995

Reel for Eilidh Shaw °

Russell Hunter
Edinburgh

© Russell Hunter 1991

Living by the Sea

Jim Sutherland
Edinburgh

©Jim Sutherland 1995

REEL

Annie Lawson

Brian McNeill
Co. Durham

© Brian McNeill 1995

REEL

Da Eye Wifie

Iain Macleod
Edinburgh

© Grian Music 1994

Pushing the Porsche

Patsy Seddon
Edinburgh

© Patsy Seddon 1995

Phil Cunningham's Reel

Aly Bain
Edinburgh

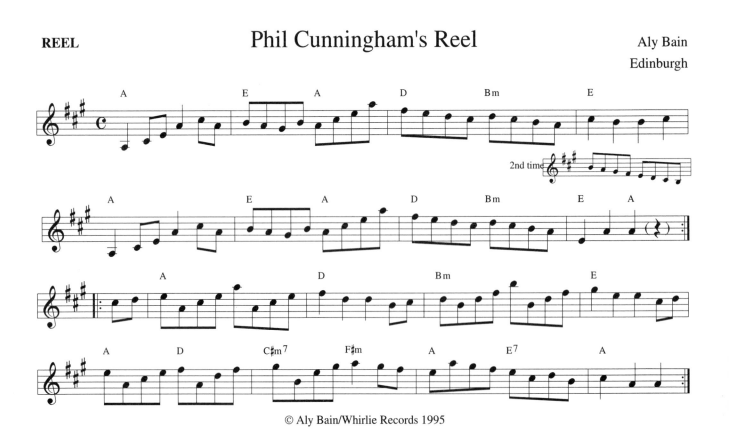

© Aly Bain/Whirlie Records 1995

T. C. Humbley's

Angus R. Grant
Edinburgh

on 2nd time through tune, play

© Angus R. Grant 1995

The Christening Piece

Stuart Eydmann
Edinburgh

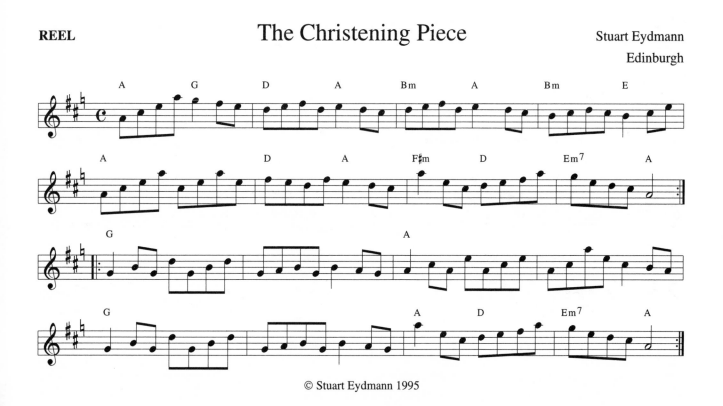

© Stuart Eydmann 1995

THE NINETIES COLLECTION

REEL

William John More

Davy Tulloch
Ayr

© Davy Tulloch 1995

REEL

The Salvation

Simon Bradley
Edinburgh

© Simon Bradley 1995

REEL

The Laggan Stockman

Gordon Pattullo
Coupar Angus

© Sunshine Music 1990

REEL

Bob McQuillin's Reel

Aly Bain
Edinburgh

© Aly Bain/Whirlie Records 1995

REEL

Bogey Broke the Back Door *

Ronnie Jamieson
Shetland

© Ronnie Jamieson 1991

REEL

The Witches of Mull

Eddie McGuire
Glasgow

*chord symbols indicate drone
accompaniment in fifths, ad libitum*

© Eddie McGuire 1993

REEL

Peats in Skow *

Karen Steven
Wick

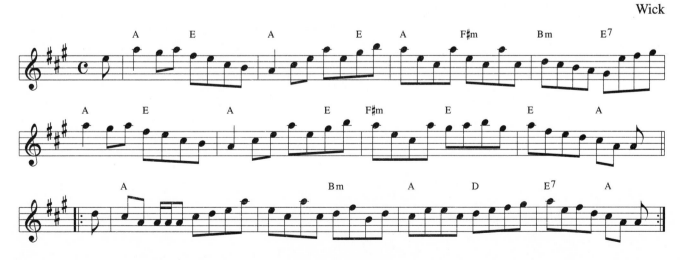

© Karen Steven 1991

THE NINETIES COLLECTION

STRATHSPEYS

Angus Grant ------------------------------------- Bert Murray --------------------- 141
Ann's Delight ----------------------------------- Kenneth Kennedy -------------- 134
Below The Aigas Dam ------------------------- Phil Cunningham --------------- 139
Birchwood-- Karen Steven -------------------- 135
Cape Spear -------------------------------------- Muriel Johnstone --------------- 138
Farewell to Number 27 ------------------------ Freeland Barbour -------------- 136
George Scott's Strathspey --------------------- Yvonne Neave ----------------- 138
Helen Margaret's Strathspey ------------------ John Dallas ---------------------- 137
Hirpling Danny --------------------------------- Hamish Small ------------------- 138
Lynsey Dewar's Strathspey -------------------- Colin Dewar -------------------- 140
Mrs. Charlotte Renton -------------------------- John Renton -------------------- 137
Mrs. Jane Chapman ---------------------------- Iain Peterson ------------------- 140
△Pamela Rose Grant---------------------------- Alasdair Fraser ----------------- 139
Stuart Strathspey ------------------------------- Tara Stuart ---------------------- 135.
The Quiet Man----------------------------------- Jim Sutherland ----------------- 142
The Royal Oak----------------------------------- Russell Hunter ----------------- 141
Welcome to Hamilton House------------------- Muriel Johnstone -------------- 136

△ CDI Track 1

George Scott's Strathspey °

Yvonne Neave
Kirriemuir

© Yvonne Neave 1991

STRATHSPEY/HORNPIPE

Ann's Delight °

Kenneth Kennedy
Bonnyrigg

© Kenneth Kennedy 1991

Stuart Strathspey °

Tara Stuart
Elgin

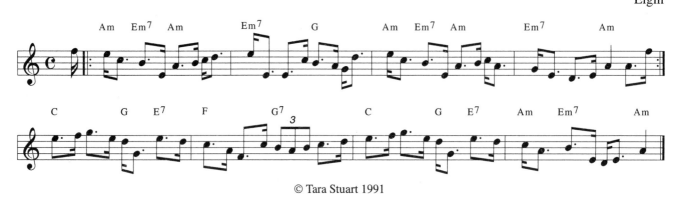

© Tara Stuart 1991

Birchwood °

Karen Steven
Wick

© Karen Steven 1991

Welcome to Hamilton House

Muriel Johnstone
Duns

© Scotscores 1993

STRATHSPEY

Farewell to Number 27

Freeland Barbour
Edinburgh

© Bonskeid Music Ltd. 1995

STRATHSPEY

Helen Margaret's Strathspey +

John Dallas

Falkirk

© John Dallas 1991

STRATHSPEY

Mrs. Charlotte Renton

John Renton

Inveraray

© Shian Music 1995

THE NINETIES COLLECTION

138

STRATHSPEY

Cape Spear

Muriel Johnstone
Duns

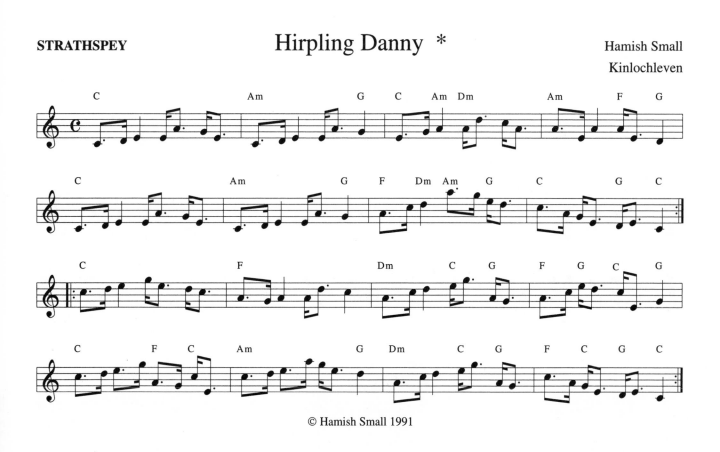

© Scotscores 1992

STRATHSPEY

Hirpling Danny *

Hamish Small
Kinlochleven

© Hamish Small 1991

STRATHSPEY

Pamela Rose Grant

Alasdair Fraser
California

© Alasdair Fraser 1995

STRATHSPEY

Below The Aigas Dam

Phil Cunningham
Beauly

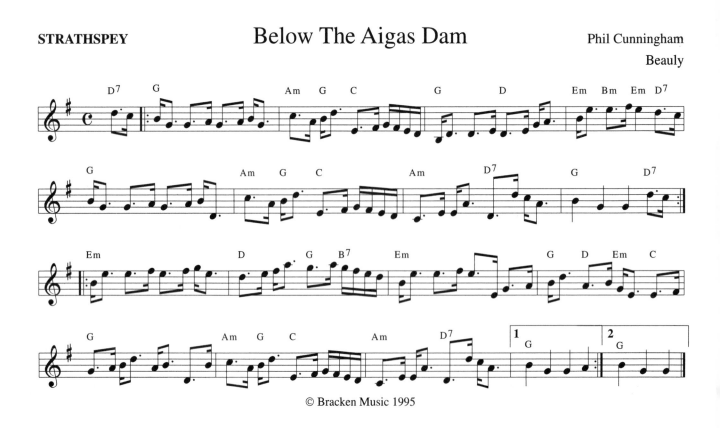

© Bracken Music 1995

Lynsey Dewar's Strathspey

Colin Dewar
Freuchie

© Bonskeid Music Ltd. 1995

STRATHSPEY

Mrs. Jane Chapman

Iain Peterson
Dollar

© Shian Music 1995

STRATHSPEY

Angus Grant °

Bert Murray
Aberdeen

© Bert Murray 1991

STRATHSPEY

The Royal Oak *

Russell Hunter
Edinburgh

© Russell Hunter 1991

STRATHSPEY

The Quiet Man

Jim Sutherland
Edinburgh

© Athol Music 1987

WALTZES

Astryd's Waltz ----------------------------------- Debbie Scott -------------------------- 148
Ba' Heid Waltz ---------------------------------- Simon Bradley ----------------------- 148
Betty M. Straughan ---------------------------- Ronald Purvis ----------------------- 149
Calum's Waltz ----------------------------------- Steven Spence ----------------------- 144
Derek and Val ----------------------------------- Ian Lowthian ------------------------ 146
Magnus Hendrichson --------------------------- Debbie Scott -------------------------- 144
The New Year Waltz --------------------------- Gordon Gunn------------------------- 145
The First Snow ---------------------------------- Charlie Soane ------------------------ 151
Violet's Waltz ----------------------------------- Bill Stewart -------------------------- 150
White Gold --------------------------------------- Brian Miller ------------------------- 147
The Wild West Waltz--------------------------- Wendy Stewart------------------------ 145

Magnus Hendrichson *

Debbie Scott
Shetland

© Debbie Scott 1991

WALTZ

Calum's Waltz

Steven Spence
Shetland

© Steven Spence 1995

The New Year Waltz °

Gordon Gunn
Wick

© Gordon Gunn 1991

Wild West Waltz

Wendy Stewart
Edinburgh

© Grian Music 1992

WALTZ

Derek and Val +

Ian Lowthian

Harrow

© Ian Lowthian 1991

THE NINETIES COLLECTION

WALTZ

White Gold *

Brian Miller
Penicuik

© Bonskeid Music Ltd. 1992

WALTZ

Ba' Heid Waltz

Simon Bradley
Edinburgh

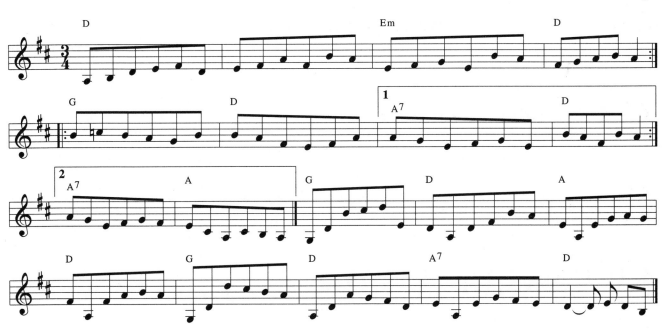

© Simon Bradley 1995

WALTZ

Astryd's Waltz *

Debbie Scott
Shetland

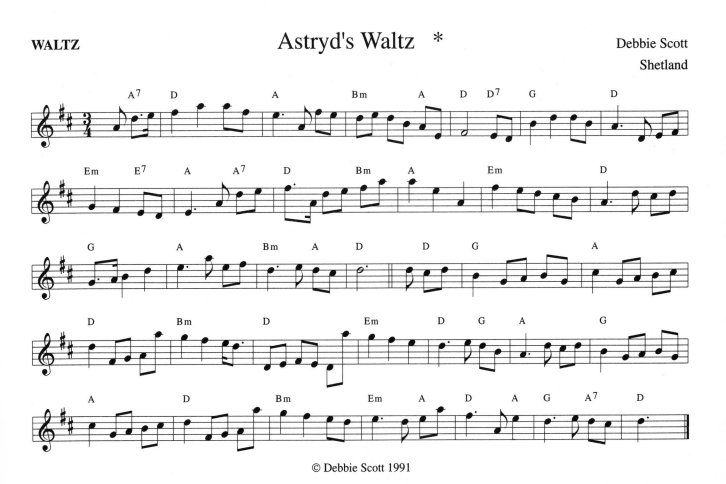

© Debbie Scott 1991

THE NINETIES COLLECTION

WALTZ

Betty M. Straughan °

Ronald Purvis
Northumberland

© Ronald Purvis 1991

Violet's Waltz °

Bill Stewart
Balfron

© Bill Stewart 1991

D.C. al Fine

WALTZ

The First Snow °

Charlie Soane
Glasgow

© Kinmor Music 1992